THE COLLAGE POEMS OF DRAFTS

RACHEL BLAU DuPLESSIS

Also by Rachel Blau DuPlessis

THE
COLLAGE
POEMS
OF
DRAFTS

RACHEL BLAU DuPLESSIS

SALT

LONDON

PUBLISHED BY SALT PUBLISHING
Acre House, 11–15 William Road , London NW1 3ER United Kingdom

Salt Publishing 2011

Printed and bound in the United States by LightningSource Inc.

Supported in part by the Pew Center for Arts & Heritage, through the Pew Fellowships in the Arts

Typeset in Paperback 11/14

ISBN 978 1 84471 758 3 paperback

1 3 5 7 9 8 6 4 2

CONTENTS

ACKNOWLEDGEMENTS   VII

MAIL ART   1
DRAFT 94: MAIL ART   3

INTRODUCTION   3

ENDNOTES   42

PRIMER   45
DRAFT CX: PRIMER   47

ACKNOWLEDGEMENTS

This book has a backstory. Because of financial and production constraints, *Pitch: Drafts 77–95* (also from Salt Publishing in 2010) could only include the black and white sections of "Draft 94: Mail Art." "Draft CX: Primer" (entirely in color) is part of my next book, the sixth in the Drafts series. The two works published together here as collage poems thus make a bridge between those two books. A publication grant from the Pew Foundation facilitated the appearance of both works as I intended them, in both color and black & white. I am deeply grateful to the Pew Foundation in every way, as well as to Salt Publishing for the honor of this special hybrid presentation, on the model of the artist's book. *The Collage Poems of Drafts* would have been impossible without this support.

The conception and some of "Mail Art" was accomplished in February 2007 on a grant from the Rockefeller Foundation that allowed me to work at Bellagio, Italy for a month. The collages and poems were completed at the National Humanities Center, North Carolina (2008–09). I extend grateful thanks to Phillip Barron of the National Humanities Center, for his technical help with the final and web presentation of this poem. I am very beholden to him for his help and for his insightful commitment to this project. In addition, to scan my work to go into the final version of this book as a whole, I received interested and expert help from the staff at the Instructional Support Center at Temple University, notably Peter Hanley. "Draft 94: Mail Art" originally appeared in *Jacket Magazine* 37; for this and many other manifestations of his support, I am quite grateful to John Tranter, the editor. "Draft CX: Primer" was composed during the summer of 2009. A few pages of "Draft CX: Primer" have been published in *Beautiful Navigator* and in *Viz: Inter-Arts* in 2010 and 2011.

MAIL ART

DRAFT 94: MAIL ART
INTRODUCTION

Mail Art is/was an international artwork activity, emerging from movements like Dada and Fluxus. It was a communication and gift exchange, before internet and email, sent through the post, in which every aspect of the communiqué (from the envelope on in) had a collage aesthetic as well as playful, verbally inventive, and jaunty elements. Among the features that I can't replicate in this work are the joking extra postage stamps often from odd countries like Canadada, the rubber stamps all over envelopes, the extra-national postal services (Fluxpost), and the textual materiality of the collage. However, by the tactic of scanning the works, some of the physical texture is retained. This work is an homage to and recollection of *Mail Art* from inside *Drafts*.

Draft 94: Mail Art

```
urce
    /fr/findresource
                /T/true
              /F/false
            /d/setdash
                /w/setlinewidth
                        /J/setlinecap
                                /j/se
```

Limen, limen "all These

woke every hour on the hour

little interrelated Things"

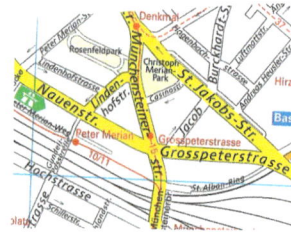

Ask the letter A
and it may tell you
What, then, and where, was the task.
to continue.

the *literally* mail:

VILLA SERBELLONI
22021 BELLAGIO (LAGO DI COMO)

anything—envelopes
scribbles
sealing
labels
certification
cancellation
delivery

correct postage ?

according to the weight of insouciance

tangled
in The long vigil
of The page

Phylacteries of simple letters bind texty
boxes to my head and arm.

But — there's also gender
twisting the leather thongs.

Really, could tell you all about me.

random lines
burning and dodging techniques
non-silver printing

a monument to any day
half-hazardly

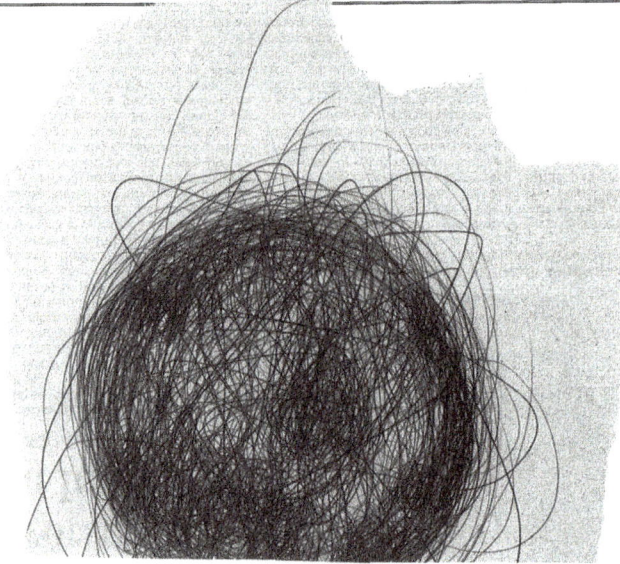

OFFICIAL PHOTO   Mo DUPLESRIS

traveling raveling reveling reveling

«ICH»

The predominance of lines was an international phenomenon

and words: Their laden socio-twisty
selves

listening differently
I got off the train and... This double function can be found in
                        as the meandering seam of the female
beginning again what

    Sonorlette bedeu.
    lockeren Zusmmen,all-encompassing development. Whereas

             de cette dimension, il n'y a rien d'autre
       à faire que de "composer", qu'on se trouve impliqué dans
            multiples that cannot
            attach the points there are
            however many hypotenuses
            one postulates, that go cross every X
            and every T, that triangulate
            even things one cannot even note.

simultaneously lead an independent existence.

Mein Interesse gilt der Suche nach deren Sonorität. Die Idee mit

    BAGGAGE IDENTIFICATION TAG

For this reason, they avoid a layered pictorial structure with

    women leaning out of the cabin window as well

    VIA
                    replaced underperforming managers,
    VIA   and redefined the company, aiming it

    VIA
    0220 702246
but it changes for every event), there are others,

en dialogue avec.

KUNST

to wrap vertige
   un
     ∧

SHIVERING AS HEAVY RAINS COME DOWN,

ALPHABETS BLOWN AT MY HEAD, PRIOR TO DEFINITION

turn AWAY from
turn AWAY from
          the buying
          the using, the destroying
          the unfulfilling

the insensate
the lack of empathy
the instrumentalizing
the damaged sensibility
"these drastic fucking times"

no grandstanding
regain!
regain!
The sun hums with a million tones, solar max in meets and bounds.

A single letter, black flake, blows back against the page.

LIFT HERE

OPEN HERE

ENGLISH

AGRICOLTURA

4166
Green Giant

AOX

BIGLIETTO VALIDO PER UNA CORSA
TICKET VALID FOR ONE TRIP

don't center anything

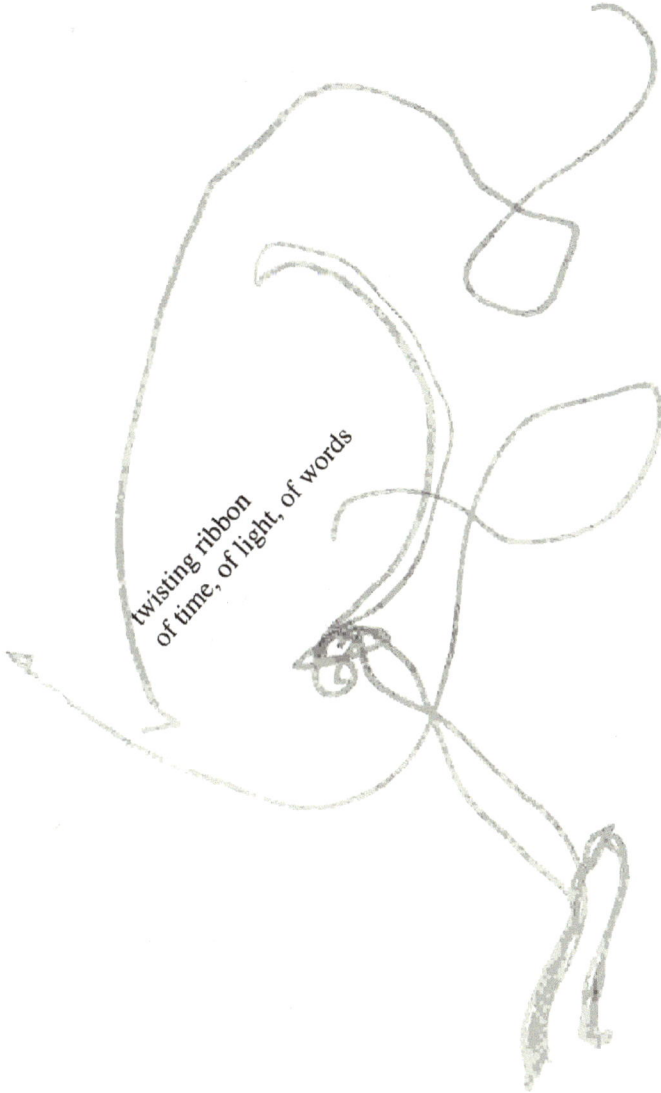

twisting ribbon
of time, of light, of words

110 WHAT IS A BOOK?

ואלו קשרים פרק חמשה עשר שבת קטו

Shabbat tractate, 115a

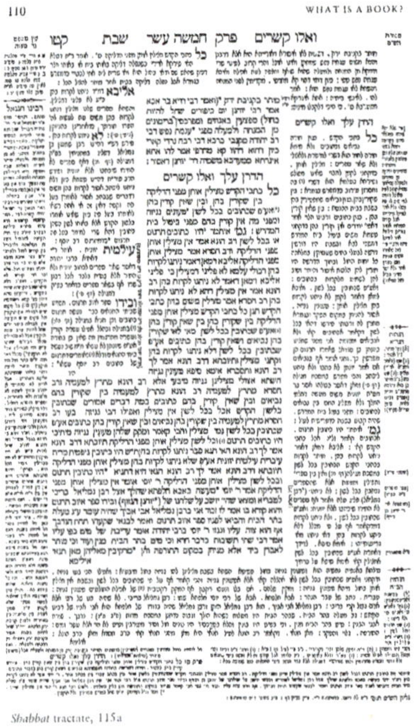

talismanic
Talmudic

230 כל כתבי פרק ששה עשר שבת

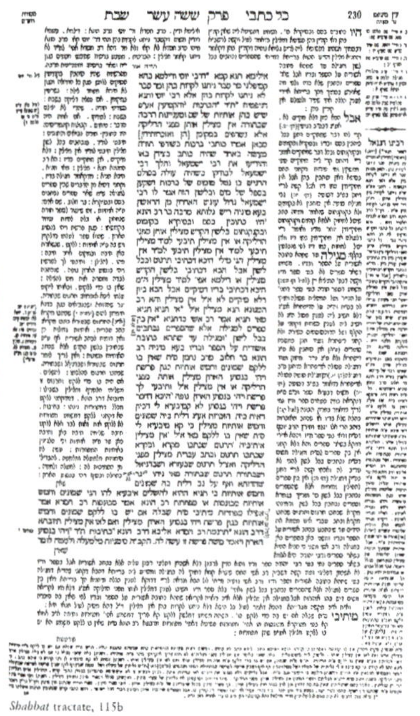

Shabbat tractate, 115b

R   EST   LESS I was late for the appointment,   was trying to map a drive to
where, where was the place I was   going? sets out the typos of excess
breakable code dismembered words What is, is. What's
            torn is laden with further burdens,
                        even if there are again 7 new days.
                        Thus one enters one's own life as a traveler.

7 new days

Even a nothing, the ur-dot
Stood
not majesty, not overview
but dot to dot, and mite to mite
 "every discomfort produces desire"
inundated in a flood of light.

Make a shape for the day.
I want the diagonal.

YYY
 If there were holes cut in this page
(not impossible)
what would be the word groups
underneath?

underneath gets better and better

The light of the day begins at one. At dawn the sun is arc-
        ky. Is askew. This is a textbook case of Bright bits, silence of the real but a glitter,
a glittering, as if sound by the side of the road. Pause. Wait. Moon-ruffled, sun-pierced,

the cloudy subject rising over the horizon or even over the mountain enters the hegemony
of political space. countdown. wonder amid the opening up of the newspaper. stalemate.

note, anyway, the motif of the snake

the little light
as if it had returned
to its own anonymity.
such mercy
mire me.

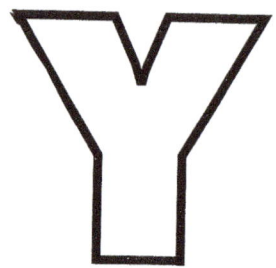

pousse

pousse

poudre   day
          ben day
          bench day
          ben la Y

peut-

(aussi)

être

Y

orphic trek bock pock littlespeck

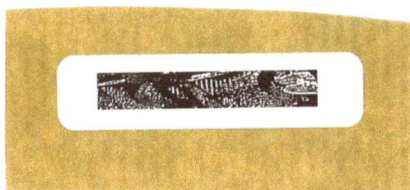

Posteitaliane

Ufficio Postale
1

10/07/2007 10.48

Prodotti Postali

P042

Basically—what do I know. Really.

I have no idea what to do except

"I enclose a Y (a fragment of RAY)."

The Theory of the Everyday

kneytch, creased and crumpled,
gone thoughts are gone
behind regrets--
Still, it's also one-third annoyance
two-thirds improper radiant sound
on the edge of almost forgetting what we came for:
Again?
Was there in fact a purpose?
Reduplicate the awkwardness!

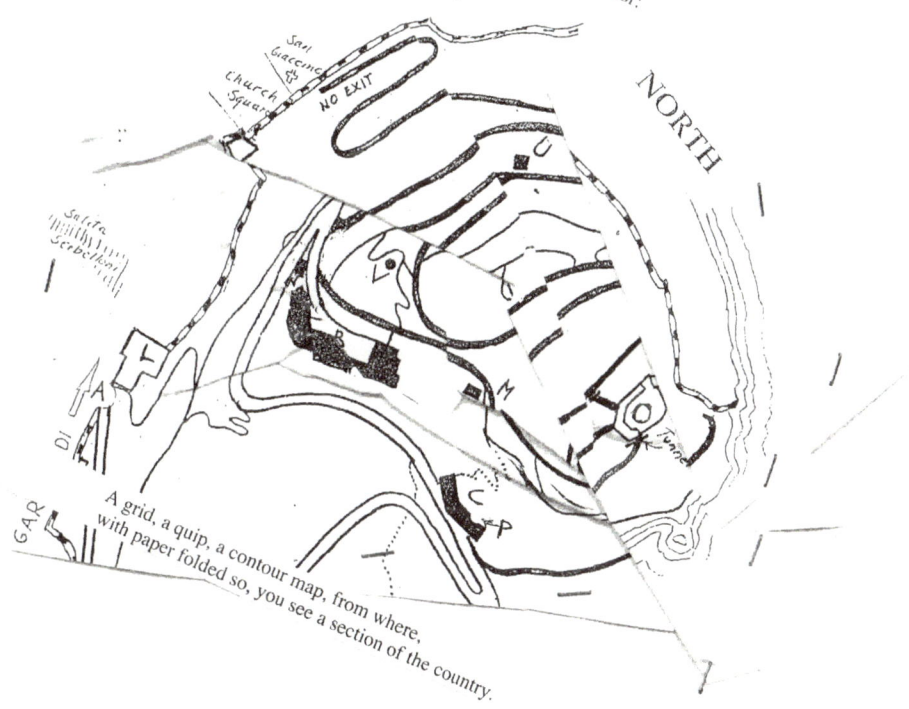

A grid, a quip, a contour map, from where,
with paper folded so, you see a section of the country.

MAKES

EIN

KUNST

PRODUKT

specifically poss ss ess ed
by not a sound but sound is the way to show it\chunck chucnk trr. usw
theoretic uhhhh
blah!

E

ARD

T

Type A
in R

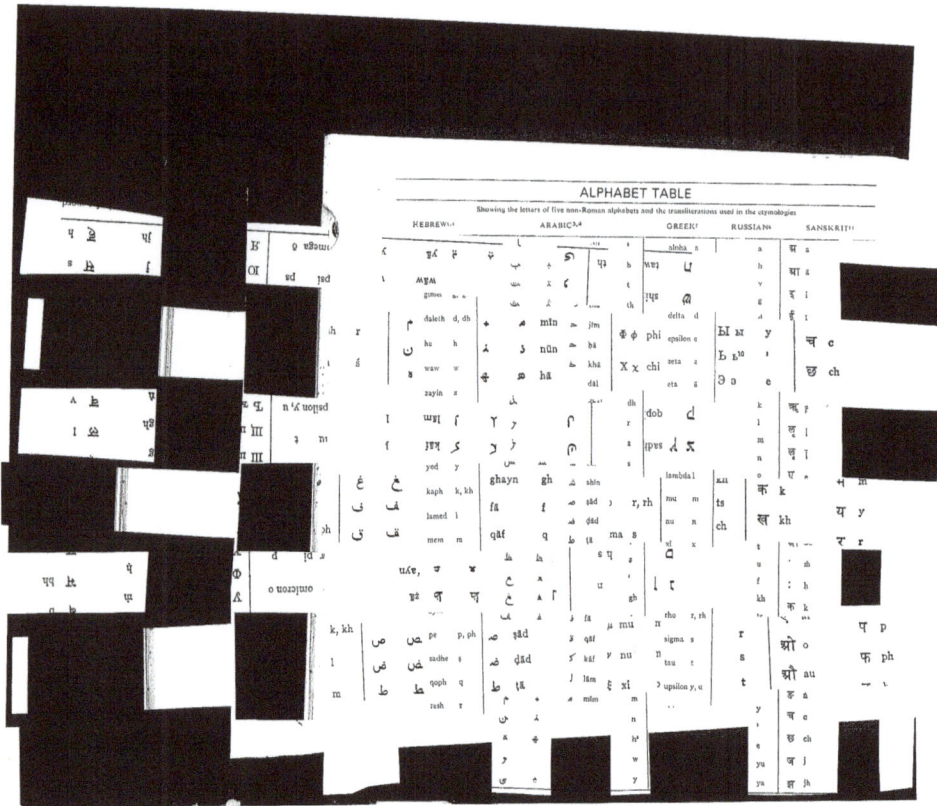

lex

and language is "social sculpture"

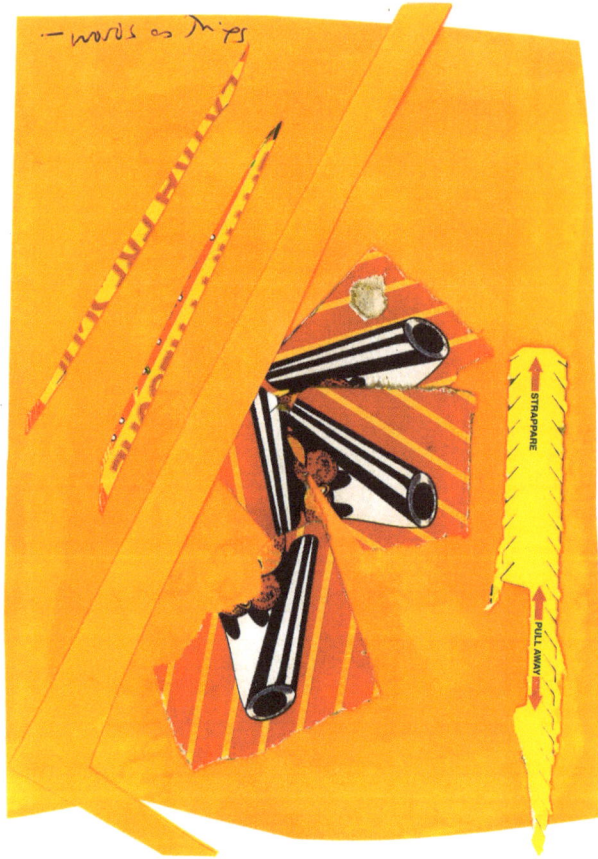

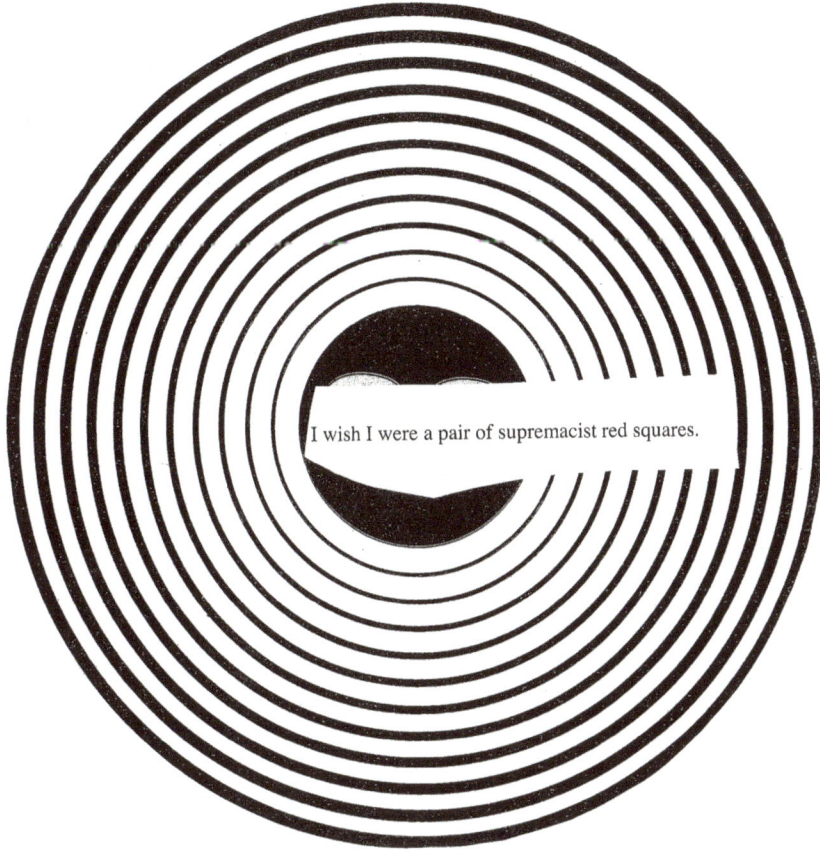

I wish I were a pair of supremacist red squares.

BLANC

exis

Perhaps translucence is a quality of erasu

exigency
necessity
agency
cadence

swollen, tender, tendus, swilling

LA LANGUE

To want the void

within the text, *yet* →

Each single word, each labile letter
opened a mini-world
from particular presence and long implication.
it was so fast, and so distracting
and sometimes saturate with pleasure
at the exactness of calibration
in the endless vast excess.

letters flew up into the space
of codes that bring things
to face themselves not just as
themselves but as also linked
to each other and to us, in air filled with
generosity.
ferocity.

where the light is

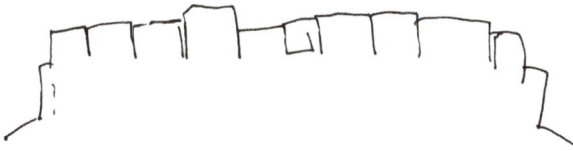

light is centered by a small black wall
capturing air in oblique folds

Babel striates the poet herself.
It's not that we do not live
precariously—the Bomb and bombs,
The war and wars,
a violent storm, a meteor strike, drought and
heartless, heedless starvation,
or the drowning of

coast-line cities--but we never
understand ourselves thereby.
Words already fail...
And once an owl crossed my path.
I wrote on this,
And so much else.
But nothing was "on"
in that old-fashioned sense.

I want to write one word here that will tell everything:

it is a ridiculous desire.

The word may be desire.

It is all words.

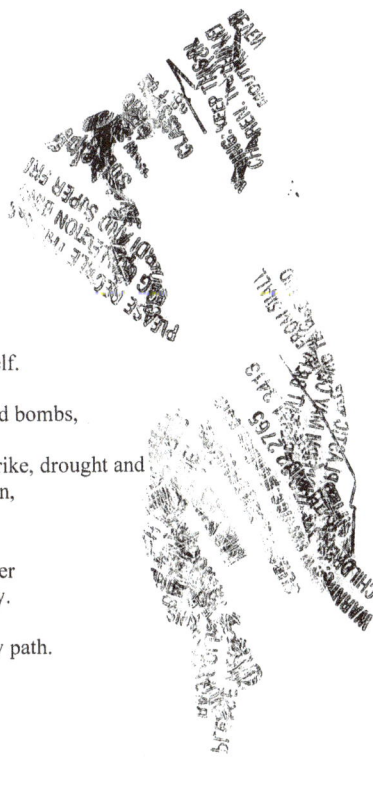

∘ ∘ ∘ =I asked the diagram what to do, and it said
"A revolution must "seize cultural power"
and then let go of it.

I'll be here my whole life
deciphering palimpsests
to find the other alphabet
one scratched in H's
and resisting serifs claimed as Law.

What you see is what you get,
is what they say.
Half the story, actually.
The other half or more
un-scene, ur-new.
How many fractions and implications
exist, exigent and excessive.
How to bring their pulses into
this.

That's the ticket.

Stuff things in the scrapbook,
Unravel cross-hatched webbings.
        Postcard ticket postcard
use the edge of the train stub

        urbanity, macchiato
elaboration, collaboration, appropriation,
        fustic quarter-sawn obstacles, debilitating heat,
and the traveler
told such a story
of the difference between gray and grey
that one almost believed her.

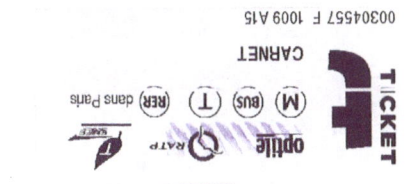

ART AS A

ART. 130/E
1000 PUNTI

STAPLE

— ← see?

ENDNOTES

Note to page 5. The letter visuals spelling MAI are designed by Zaugg, from the Remy Zaugg exhibition catalog, a work called "Vom Tod II," 1999/2002/2004, from the Zentrum Paul Klee, Bern.

Note to page 6: "all these little interrelated things" stated by Ray Johnson, as cited by Mason Klein in *Ray Johnson: Correspondences*, ed. Donna De Salvo and Catherine Gudis. Columbus, Ohio: Wexner Center for the Arts and Paris: Flammarion, 1999, 55.

Note to page 10: The visual in "Official Photo" is the hairball advertising the *International Herald Tribune*, appearing in Sat-Sun. Feb 3, 2007, on 5.

Note to page 11: The page beginning "The predominance of lines was an international . . ." has several sources to credit. Anita Haldemann wrote the art historical text, from her brochure for the exposition "Neoclassicism to Early Modernism, Positions of Drawing in the 19th Century," Kunstmuseum Basel in the Kupferstichkabinett. The composer Junghae Lee wrote the text in German as a description of her "Sonorletten fur Kalviertrio mit Elektronik (2006)" heard at Gare du Nord concert space, in Basel. The French comes from a brochure from the Beyeler Museum in Basel. All Basel materials are indebted to the hospitality of Anne Blonstein.

Note to page 13: Uses the alphabet table from Webster's Ninth *New Collegiate Dictionary*. Springfield, MA: Merriam-Webster, Inc., 1986, p. 74.

Note to page 18: The Hebrew text is cited/ photocopied from *The Burnt Book: Reading the Talmud* by Marc-Alan Ouaknin, trans. Llewellyn Brown, Princeton: Princeton University Press, 1995, 110–111.

Note to page 24: "I enclose a Y . . ." Ray Johnson, *The Paper Snake*. New York: Something Else Press, 1965, n.p.

Note to page 30: Uses the alphabet table from Webster's Ninth *New Collegiate Dictionary*. Springfield, MA: Merriam-Webster, Inc., 1986, p. 74.

Note to page 31: Includes a citation from Joseph Beuys: and language is "social sculpture." Cited in a museum label: Biennale in Sydney, Summer 2008.

Note to page 35: The definitions of tongue
are from Webster's Ninth *New Collegiate
Dictionary*. Springfield, MA: Merriam-
Webster, Inc., 1986, 1242.

PRIMER

DRAFT CX: PRIMER

Letters, a preface.

     to the matted mast of alphabet

This is a work from bursts of the visual in the verbal, and round about again, verse visa. This is a work primed with letters, with colors, read and seen, red and scene, the magic and oddity of daily life ripped to bits

                  rotting and steaming, filled with red-tipped worms. Just the daily, as in dated blocks. fluttering letter-farfalle un-cocooned. To see the letters sweetly, but with surge behind them. This is creation, combustible, sensuous, pleasures giving pleasure. Rebar of the infrastructure. The Alpha and Omega. A wry powerful wraith. Pairing letters, paring words, peering over the A byss, the B byss of feather hemp pot (poet) determinatives. As in m no am em, O, on the SE corner to BE. HHow does one learn to see the difference, in a new alphabet—the minrness of the detail. A dot, a yod-like qshift or change and difference, alteration, shift, palette sounded here and there. (h) (h) (h) (h) plus X, its pluck and jube.

Crackle sounds and sonorities. Each letter (R. C. M.) an epistle TO the one who looks at them. *as if the letters, touching, read the word, the word the text.* Gripping each other. N as in begin. A is followed by Y. Some letters fold over themselves, facing each others' halves: H. T. W. Perhaps O. The letters rise as if propelled on smoke, the leaves burn, the flecks of autumn go to ash; this book dissolves into its making. Q.V. to all of it.

There is packing. There is oddity. There is conjunction. There's even Qwerty. Pessoa's was Azerty.
And there we are again—the alphabet. For the n-th time
The books compost. The letters detach. A again, again they say, for apple. The appeal and appel. Apt. The W of Cassiopeia now an M. And Zone. This is very odd. UneXpected. Which is just to say: This Book is one of them, it is.

Some of it is funny. The fframed, the is-lated, the sudden brought together with others of the same. Of that ilk. Ilk of ilkiness. Honestly—the letters NSEW. Cardinals. Who knew? O and I are, they say, the most (poetic)™. This letter is life, iota-iota. A dot is as extensive as π wherein all the numbers, unrepeating, are gathered to a point. En plus, E, Etc. These are letters and they are tinged with what they are. R.

The N's and Y's and Xing place and R's dominate
but sometimes R is dropped from the work
I mean from the word
with odd
e-sults.

As they tumble up their alphabetic stair, as the petal hits the mettle, I go down the passage into a mirroring zone. It is as if these made themselves. They wanted to be. Faced with the bright alphabet, the letters want to say themselves, their bits. Open the packages! Turn it all inside out! A process of scraping, of ripping, of pasting. Wanting the insides of things, their undersides. The package inside out. The layers of pressing. The cardboard. Mite and mote. It's being like that.

They glean, they unpack and layer, they are a little thick, they deturn images, they frame and reframe the debris. They gleam.

And they reach and touch, and I am in their house.
We meet, collapse and tumble.
One raucous interface,
porous, yod to yod, one and one,
and each to each.

DECEMBER 2009 & AUGUST 2010

all these libations include APPLE.

how many ways to get this information across?

Auras of both words and things,
of Colors, shapes and edges fall.

It's just a primer—pedagogical.

'A' ABD. JUNE 09/ NOV 09

Babel striates the poet herself
B was P.
Bread was Pane.
Brot was Pain.

'B' RBD Jul 09 & Nov 09

Count a
won too tree
furor avid sex
plait intensity nigh
tint a TIN
out.

RBD June 09 'C' Nov 09

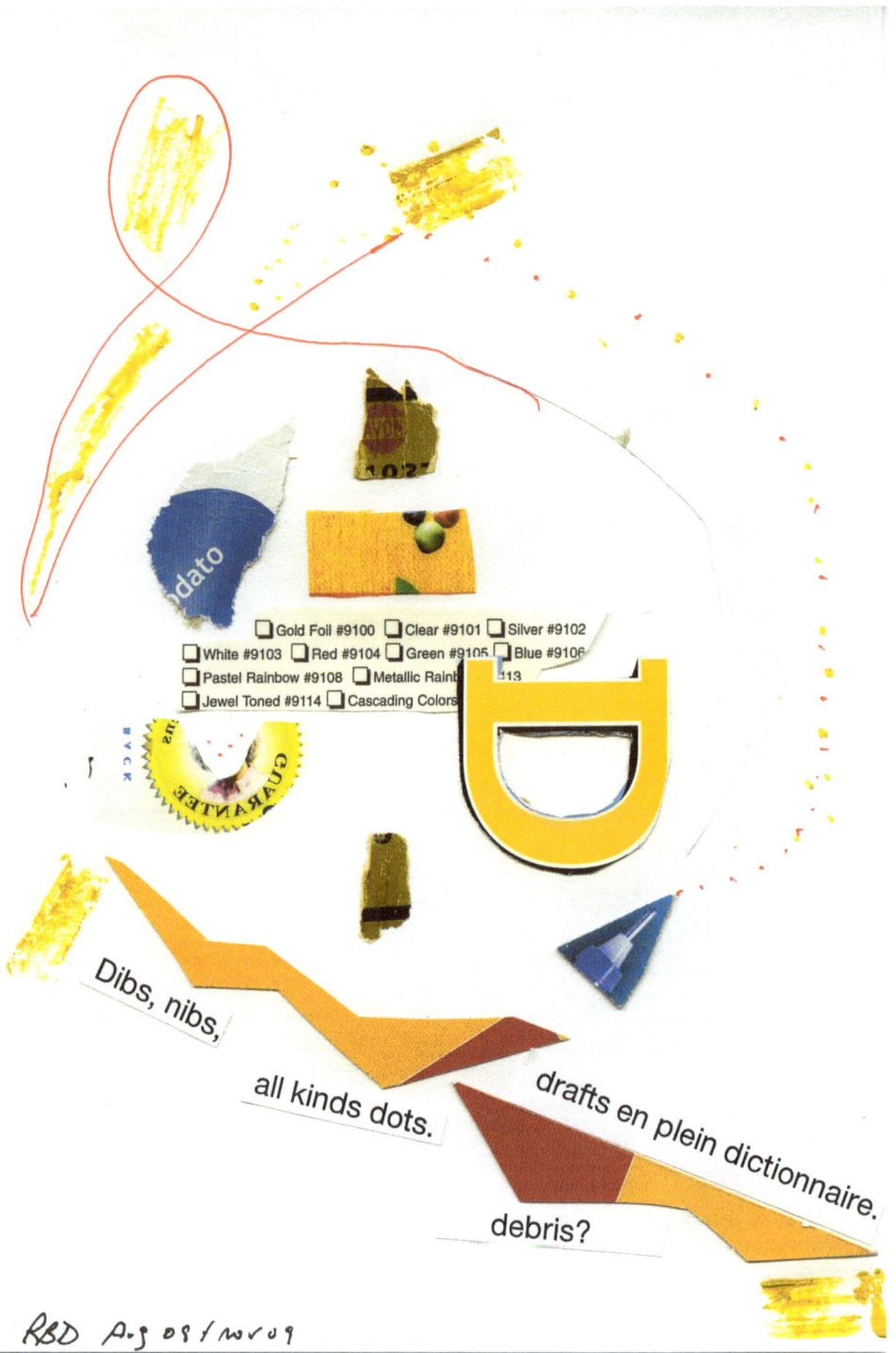

Gold Foil #9100   Clear #9101   Silver #9102
White #9103   Red #9104   Green #9105   Blue #9106
Pastel Rainbow #9108   Metallic Rainbow 113
Jewel Toned #9114   Cascading Colors

Dibs, nibs,

all kinds dots.

drafts en plein dictionnaire.

debris?

'D' RBD A.g 08/nov09

One-third disgruntlement two-thirds radiant practices.

'E' RBD June 09/Nov

for

Too Fast Too Fast 2
Simple 2 ~~IMQ~~ 2 Simple
Too Fast To Fast Too

Fast Fast

Much) too

Simple st Too

Fast Really

too Fe it f to fast

It is much too Too Fast

2 Simple too Jos F this

pen is running out running out

'F' RBD June 09

PRODUZIONE CERTIFICATA

AD 172566 A
CONSORZIO

CERMET
PIANO ALL
IT 2002-03

I missed the second ringing G in Dinggedicht.

Mischancing

UNIVERSITA' DI CAMERINO

BIBLIOTECA GIURI

NUMERO DI
INGRESSO   122595

È IL MIO TURNO

G02

TIRARE

that clunking
sonorous gleam
of thing and poem
of poem and thing
and thing and song.

'g' RSD Jul 09 · Nov 09

The house flew through the air
and landed on the lot.

years after she died

Is this house large enough
to house this plot?

I beg for talking a little

to my mother's handkerchief

'H' RBD June 09 · Nov 09

Rebar codes
reinforce concrete.
Any one is little here
witless witness,
but held up very solidly
in the structure.

right in a jiff.

whatever a jiff is

more precarious

than a circus.

'J' RBD Aug 09·nov 09

First there's babies
(maybes)

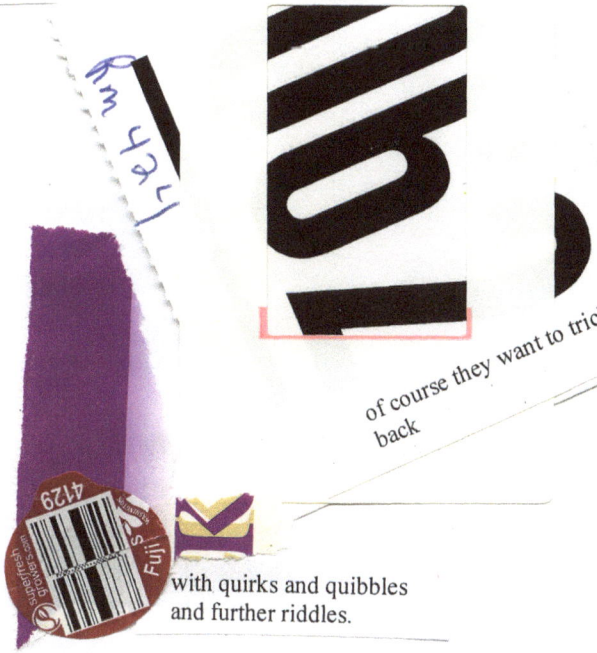

of course they want to trick you
back

with quirks and quibbles
and further riddles.

4129
Fuji
superfresh
prowls.com

'K' RBD Ma 09 · NN 09

SUCH A LOT TO DO, THUS

LONGEN FOLK TO GOON

CHECK

ON PILGRIMAGES.

'L' RBD June 09 · Nov 09

"M' vertical R30 Aus 09

That loop in time between
and "postponed"
which is now.

"N" RBD June 09

Hottest orange penny moon resents
its growing morph into the phase of darkness.

'O' RBD Aug 09 · Nov 09

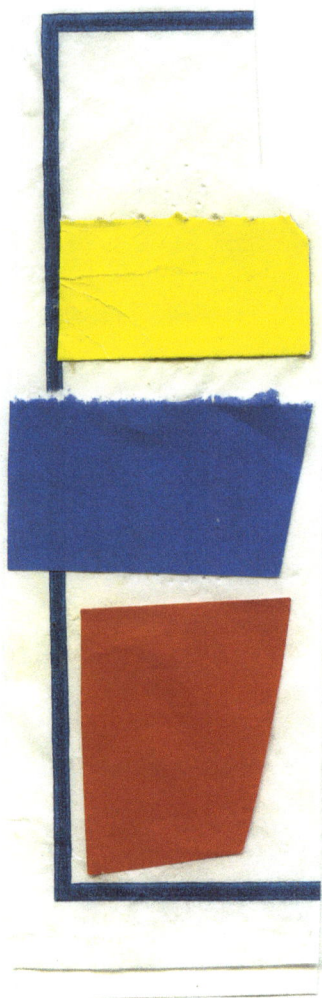

Somewhere
between recto and verso
somewhere
between odd and even
all bets are off.

'P' RSD July 09· NOV 09

'Q' RBD July 09

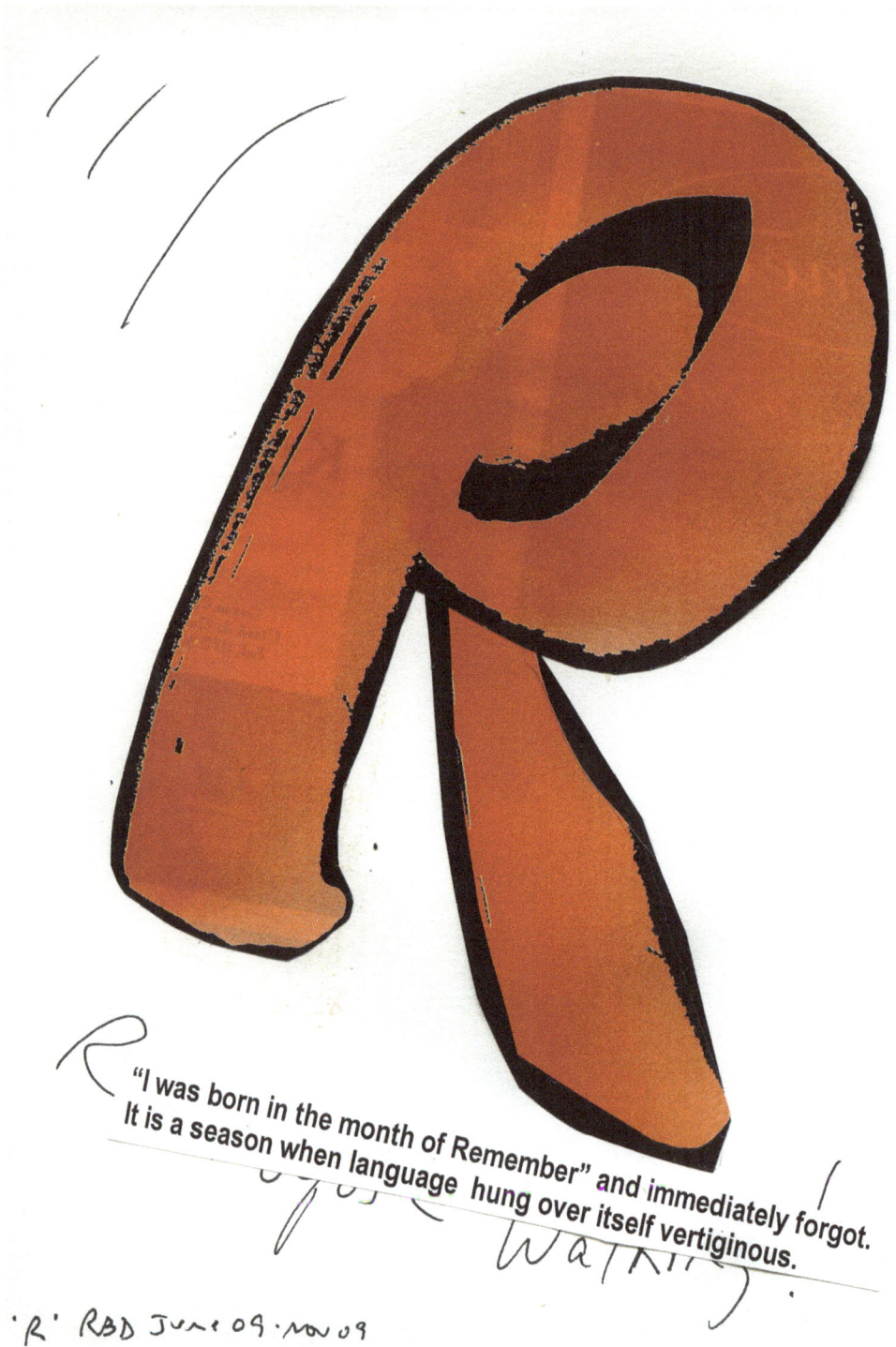

"I was born in the month of Remember" and immediately forgot.
It is a season when language hung over itself vertiginous.

'R' RBD Jun 09 · Nov 09

Salt and clouds and sky.
Are veiled and become silent.

TTILE   **TTILLE**

title and little   match up.

'T' RBD Jul, 09. Nov 09

'U' RBD Aug. Nov 2009

One hinge broke, though the other held
paper spilled through the edge of lock
from the secret valise.

49

The void and the vide
the vide and the void
fell out.

to the lost

to the stopped

watch,

A prelude

It's a lifetime,

watch,

light time.

If this is the whole world,

why feel exile in it?

'X' RBD Jul. 09. Nov 09

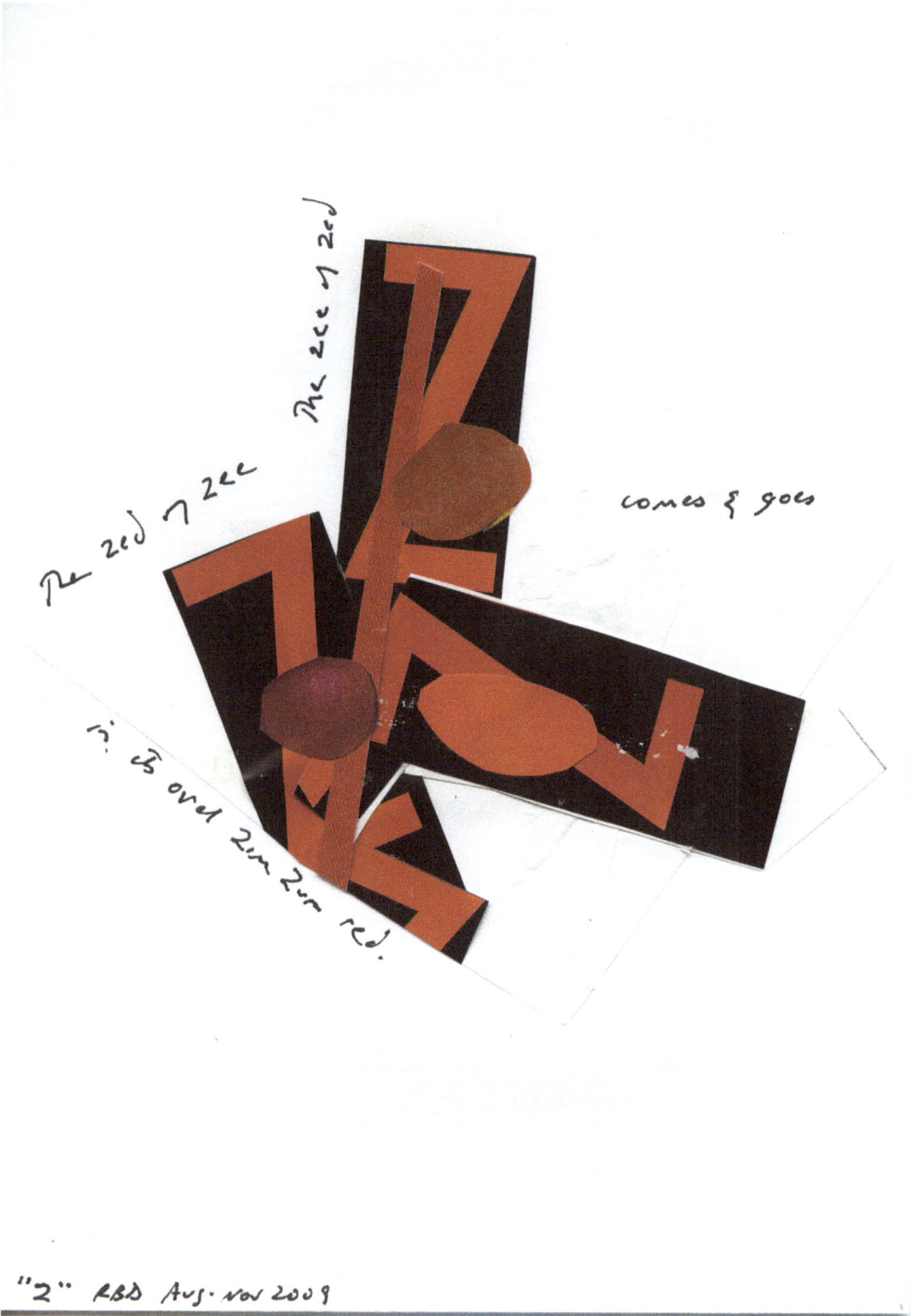

The zee of zed

The zed of zee

comes & goes

is over zoom zoom red.

"Z" RBD Aug. Nov 2009

Thanks

to The

Alphabet

Notes to Draft CX: The letters were taken from advertising and magazines. In the interests of not violating the copyrights of distinctive logos, credit should be given to Petruzzi, industria grafica in Italy, from whom their initial "P" was taken for my "R" (along with some other of the letters, like Z) and also to Golf Digest for the "D" I use.

www.ingramcontent.com/pod-product-compliance
Lightning Source LLC
Chambersburg PA
CBHW061059090426
42742CB00003B/97